All About Pets
MINECRAFT
Fun-Schooling
JOURNAL

12 Important & Interesting Subjects
Homeschooling Curriculum

WWW.FUNSCHOOLINGBOOKS.COM

This Curriculum Covers:

- Reading

- Handwriting

- Creative Writing

- Spelling

- Classical Music

- Mathematics

- Science

- History

- Art & Drawing

- Library Skills

- Unit Studies

- Logic Games

MY NAME:

Age: Date:

By:

Susannah Autumn Brown, Anna Kidalova,
Sarah Janisse Brown & Alexandra Bretush

We use the Dyslexie Font by Christian Boer

The Thinking Tree Publishing Company, LLC

FUNSchoolingBooks.com

ACTION STEPS:

1. Go to the library or bookstore.

2. Bring home a stack of at least Six interesting books about pets.

3. You will also need a math, science and history book.

4. Choose books that have diagrams, photos, instructions and illustrations.

SCHOOL SUPPLIES NEEDED:

Pencils, Colored Pencils

& Gel Pens.

GO TO THE LIBRARY AND CHOOSE SIX BOOKS.

1. Write down the titles on each book cover below.

2. Keep your stack of books in a safe place so you can read a few pages from your books daily.

3. Ask your teacher how many pages to do each day in this Journal. Five to eight pages is normal for kids your age.

MY LIBRARY BOOKS:

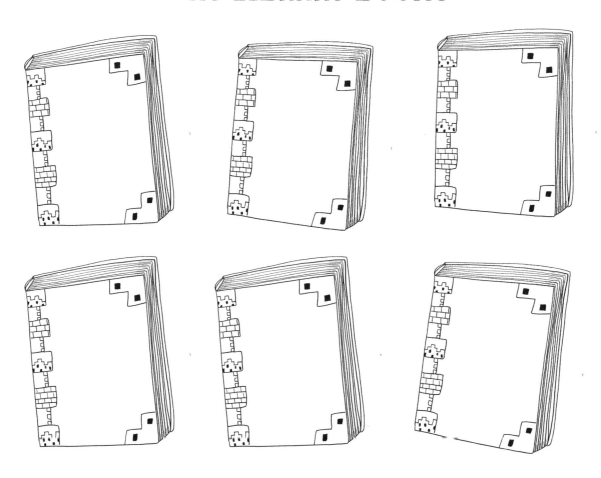

MY HOMESCHOOLING CURRICULUM:

SCIENCE:

MATH:

HISTORY:

You may choose new books any time.
Flip to the back for more book pages.
Keep all your books in a basket
with your pens and pencils.

I LOVE PETS

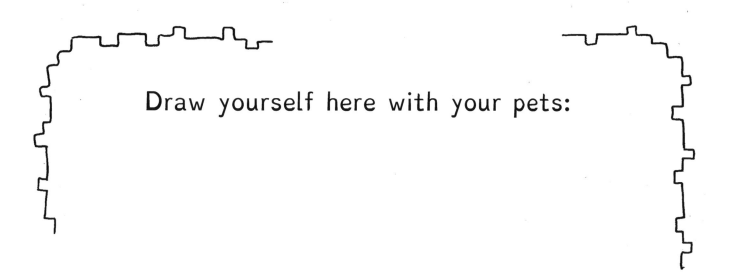

Draw yourself here with your pets:

FIVE FACTS ABOUT ME:

1. _____

2. _____

3. _____

4. _____

5. _____

Ask your teacher to help you decide how many books to read from each day. #_____

READING TIME

Write and draw about what you are reading.

ORIGAMI CHALLENGE
CAN YOU MAKE THIS ANIMAL?

Set a timer.

Minutes:_____   Seconds:_____

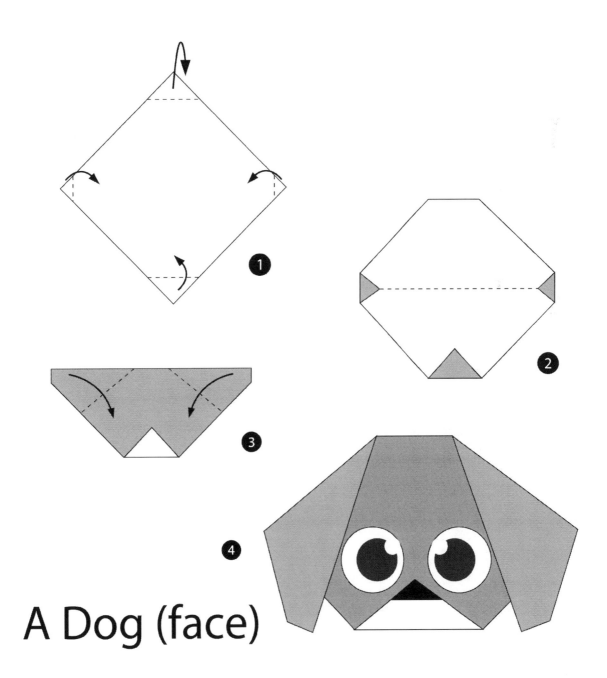

A Dog (face)

MINECRAFT

BUILDING CHALLENGE

Design and build a home for a pet in your Minecraft world, with Lego, or in real life.

Just for Fun!

STORY WRITING TIME

If you can't think and write at the same time, record your story or ask someone older for help.

Title:

_____

Names & Descriptions of Characters:

_____
_____
_____
_____
_____

Base your story on the picture to the left.

_____
_____
_____
_____
_____
_____
_____
_____
_____
_____
_____
_____
_____
_____
_____
_____
_____

DRAW ME

DRAW ME

PET TRACKS

HOW MANY PET TRACKS CAN YOU DRAW?

Coloring Time!

Draw the Missing Part

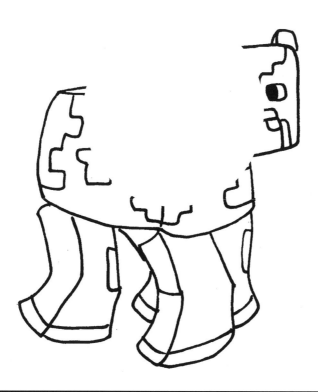

SPELLING TIME

Choose a Letter: ___

Find 15 words that begin or end with that letter.

Five Nouns:

_____

_____

_____

_____

Five Adjectives:

_____

_____

_____

_____

_____

Three pets:

_____

_____

_____

Two Verbs:

_____

_____

Write a silly story, poem, song or play using words from your spelling list.

_____

_____

_____

_____

_____

_____

_____

_____

_____

_____

_____

_____

_____

_____

_____

_____

_____

_____

CREATE A COMIC STRIP

Use your spelling words.

WHAT DID YOU LEARN ABOUT HISTORY TODAY?

_____
_____
_____
_____
_____
_____
_____
_____
_____
_____

WHAT DID YOU LEARN ABOUT SCIENCE TODAY?

_____
_____
_____
_____
_____
_____
_____

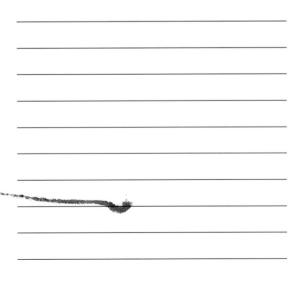

28

PETS AROUND THE WORLD

CHOOSE A POPULAR PET FROM ANOTHER COUNTRY: _____

WHERE IN THE WORLD IS THIS PET POPULAR?

FUN FACTS:

DRAW THE PET:

Today's Date:

_____

READING TIME

Write and draw about what you are reading.

LISTENING TIME

CLASSICAL MUSIC & LITERATURE

Today's Date:_____

Listen to an audio book or classical music.

Draw and doodle below.

I am listening to: _____

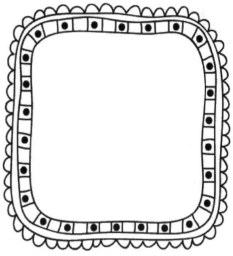

32

FIELD TRIPS & BACKYARD SCIENCE

Go somewhere and draw what you see! Look for pets.

If you can't go very far, go to a park or your own backyard.

Today's Date: _____

Today I Saw: _____

_____

_____

_____

Trace & Color

Coloring Time!

SPELLING TIME

Choose a Letter: ___

Find 15 words that begin or end with that letter.

Five Nouns:

_____

_____

_____

_____

Five Adjectives:

_____

_____

_____

_____

Three pets:

_____

_____

_____

Two Verbs:

_____

_____

Write a silly story, poem, song or play using words from your spelling list.

_____

_____

_____

_____

_____

_____

_____

_____

_____

_____

_____

_____

_____

_____

_____

_____

CREATE A COMIC STRIP

Use your spelling words.

Today's Date:

_____

Write and draw about what you are reading.

Just for Fun!

MINECRAFT

BUILDING CHALLENGE

Design and build a home for a pet in your Minecraft world, with Lego, or in real life.

LISTENING TIME

CLASSICAL MUSIC & LITERATURE

Today's Date:_____

Listen to an audio book or classical music.

Draw and doodle below.

I am listening to: _____

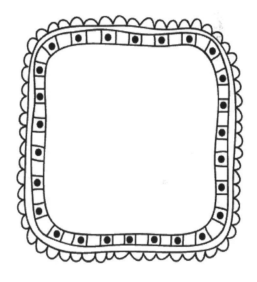

WHAT DID YOU LEARN ABOUT HISTORY TODAY?

WHAT DID YOU LEARN ABOUT SCIENCE TODAY?

PETS AROUND THE WORLD

CHOOSE A POPULAR PET FROM ANOTHER COUNTRY: _____

WHERE IN THE WORLD IS THIS PET POPULAR?

FUN FACTS:

DRAW THE PET:

Today's Date:
_____

READING TIME

Write and draw about
what you are reading.

CURSIVE WRITING PRACTICE

FIELD TRIPS & BACKYARD SCIENCE

Go somewhere and draw what you see! Look for pets.

If you can't go very far, go to a park or your own backyard.

Today's Date: _____

Today I Saw: _____

_____

_____

_____

MOVIE TIME

Watch a movie or documentary about pets.

TITLE:_____

RATING:

ORIGAMI CHALLENGE
CAN YOU MAKE THIS ANIMAL?

Set a timer.

Minutes:_____   Seconds:_____

MOUSE

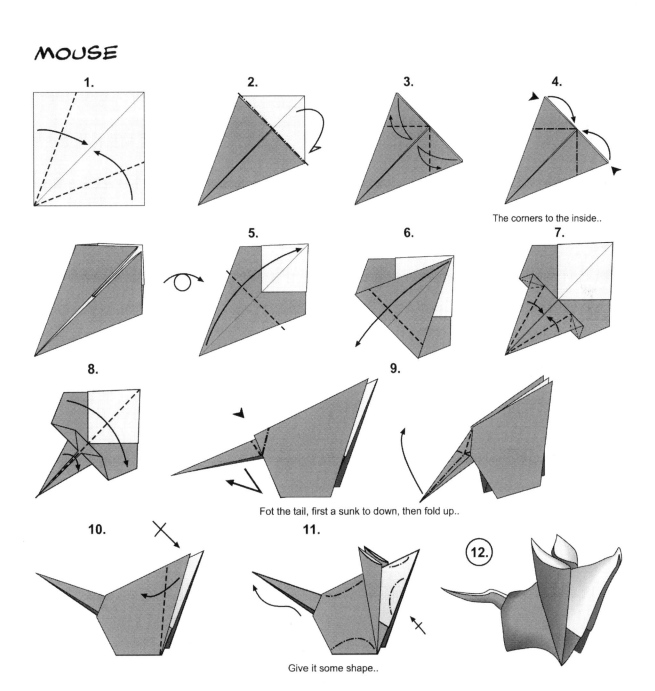

The corners to the inside..

Fot the tail, first a sunk to down, then fold up..

Give it some shape..

Coloring Time!

Draw the Missing Part

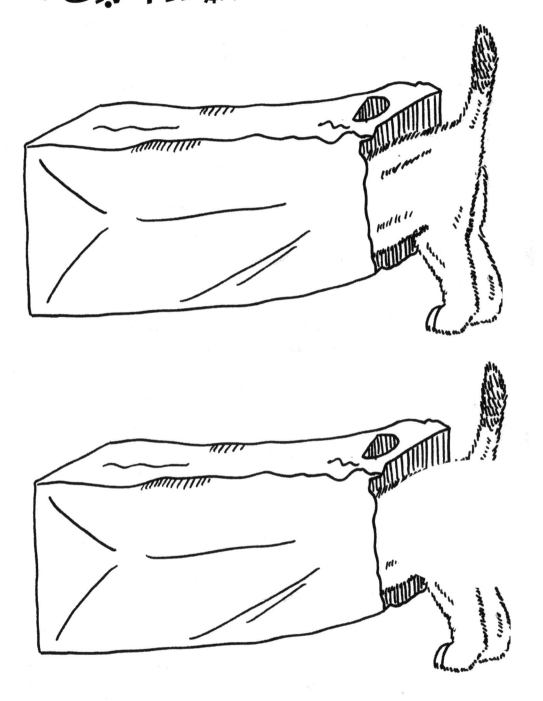

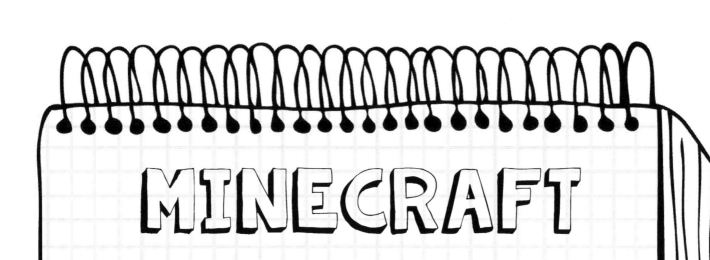

MINECRAFT

BUILDING CHALLENGE

Design and build a home for a pet in your Minecraft world, with Lego, or in real life.

PET QUIZ

I am _____

I live in _____

I like to eat _____

My friends are _____

STORY WRITING TIME

If you can't think and write at the same time, record your story or ask someone older for help.

Title:

_____

Names & Descriptions of Characters:

_____

_____

_____

_____

_____

Base your story on the picture to the left.

_____

_____

_____

_____

_____

_____

_____

_____

_____

_____

_____

_____

_____

_____

_____

_____

_____

SPELLING TIME

Choose a Letter: ____

Find 15 words that begin or end with that letter.

Five Nouns:

_____

_____

_____

_____

Five Adjectives:

_____

_____

_____

_____

_____

Three pets:

_____

_____

_____

Two Verbs:

_____

_____

Write a silly story, poem, song or play

using words from your spelling list.

_____

_____

_____

_____

_____

_____

_____

_____

_____

_____

_____

_____

_____

_____

_____

_____

CREATE A COMIC STRIP

Use your spelling words.

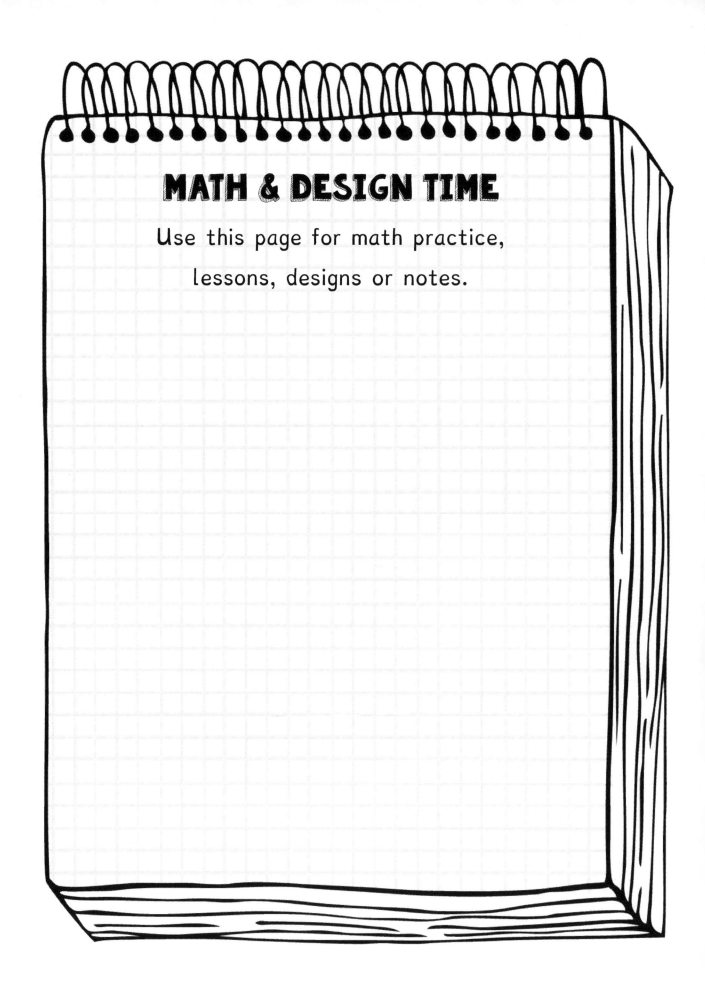

MATH & DESIGN TIME

Use this page for math practice,
lessons, designs or notes.

CURSIVE WRITING PRACTICE

What am I Thinking?

SPELLING TIME

Choose a Pet

_____

Look in your books for 10 words that have some of the same letters as this pet.

1._____

2._____

3._____

4._____

5._____

6._____

7._____

8._____

9._____

10._____

Today's
Date:

TO-DO LIST

1._____

2._____

3._____

4._____

How are you
FEELING TODAY?

Draw a Pet

CREATIVE WRITING

Write a short story about this picture. Ask someone
older to help you write the words.

WHAT DID YOU LEARN ABOUT HISTORY TODAY?

WHAT DID YOU LEARN ABOUT SCIENCE TODAY?

PETS AROUND THE WORLD

CHOOSE A POPULAR PET FROM ANOTHER COUNTRY: _____

WHERE IN THE WORLD IS THIS PET POPULAR?

FUN FACTS:

DRAW THE PET:

Trace & Color

Today's Date:
_____

READING TIME

Write and draw about what you are reading.

MINECRAFT

BUILDING CHALLENGE

Design and build a home for a pet in your Minecraft world, with Lego, or in real life.

MOVIE TIME

Watch a movie or documentary about pets.

TITLE:_____

RATING:

Draw Your Favorite Scenes:

ORIGAMI CHALLENGE
CAN YOU MAKE THIS ANIMAL?

Set a timer.

Minutes:_____   Seconds:_____

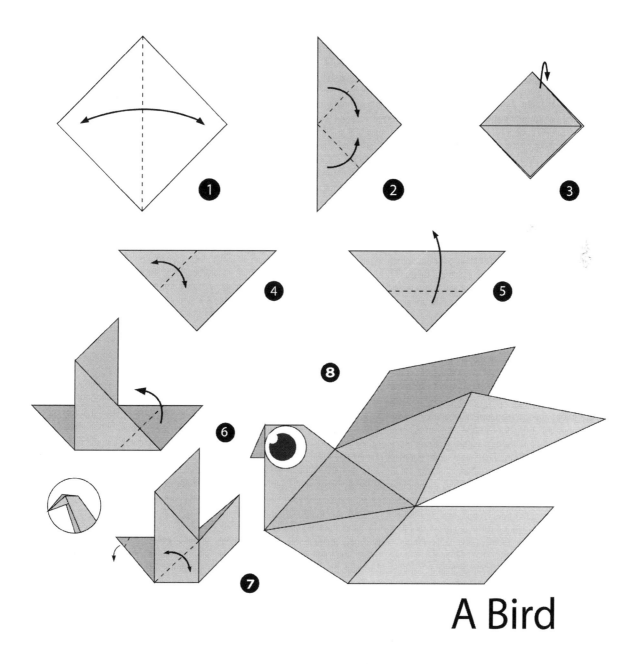

A Bird

Coloring Time!

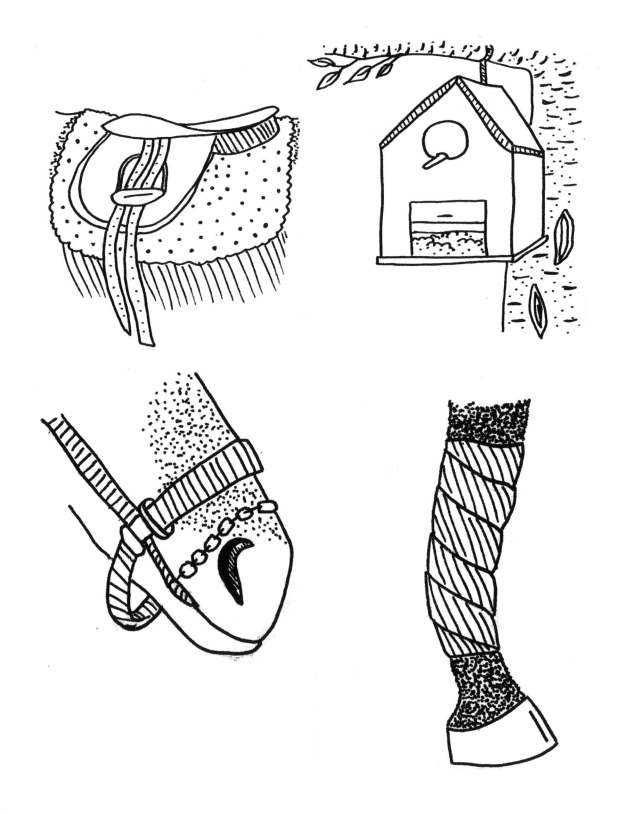

Draw the Missing Part

MINECRAFT

BUILDING CHALLENGE

Design and build a home for a pet in your
Minecraft world, with Lego, or in real life.

Just for Fun!

SPELLING TIME

Choose a Pet

_____

Look in your books for 10 words that have some of the same letters as this pet.

1._____

2._____

3._____

4._____

5._____

6._____

7._____

8._____

9._____

10._____

FIELD TRIPS & BACKYARD SCIENCE

Go somewhere and draw what you see! Look for pets.

If you can't go very far, go to a park or your own backyard.

Today's Date: _____

Today I Saw: _____

_____

_____

_____

SPELLING TIME

Choose a Letter: ___

Find 15 words that begin or end with that letter.

Five Nouns:

_____

_____

_____

_____

Five Adjectives:

_____

_____

_____

_____

_____

Three pets:

_____

_____

_____

Two Verbs:

_____

_____

Write a silly story, poem, song or play

using words from your spelling list.

_____

_____

_____

_____

_____

_____

_____

_____

_____

_____

_____

_____

_____

_____

_____

_____

_____

CREATE A COMIC STRIP

Use your spelling words.

Today's Date:

_____

READING TIME

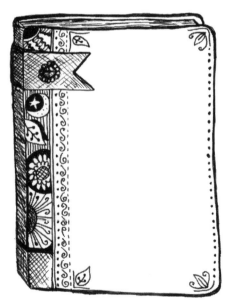

Write and draw about what you are reading.

COPYWORK

Copy a paragraph from one of your library books.

TITLE: _____ Page#_____

_____

_____

_____

_____

_____

DRAWING TIME

Copy an illustration from one of your books.

PIXEL ART

Ideas & Inspiration

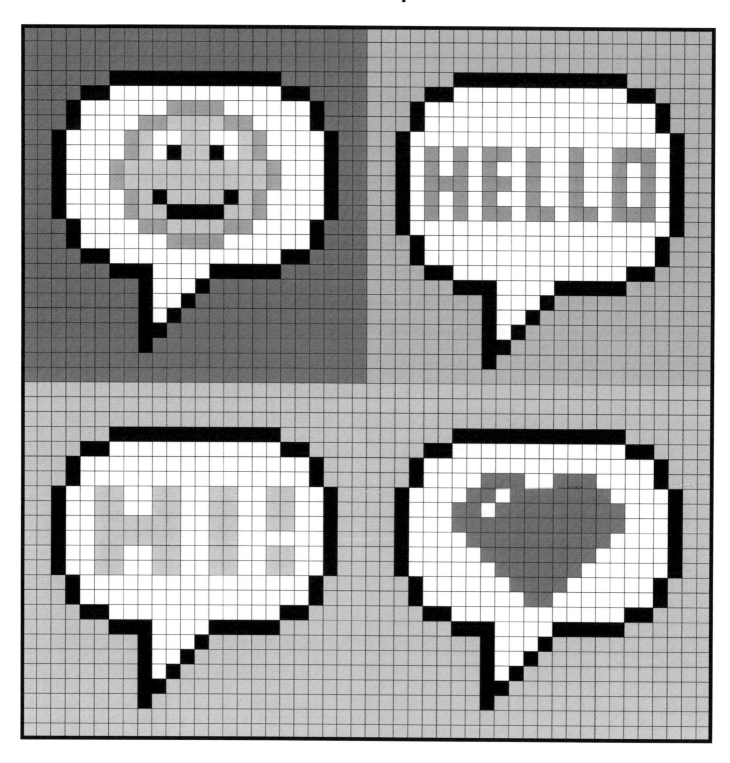

PIXEL ART

Create Your Own Pixel Design

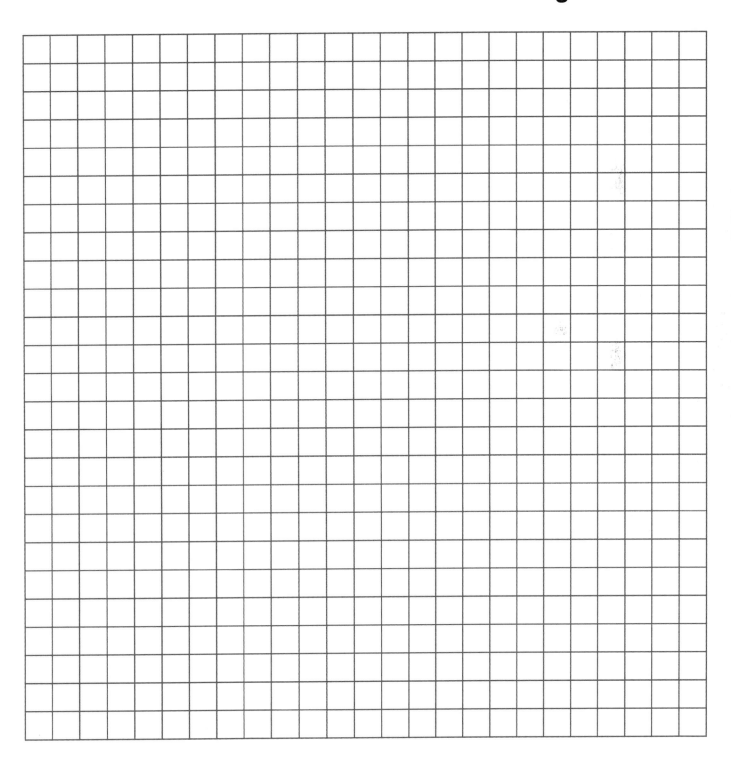

WHAT DID YOU LEARN ABOUT HISTORY TODAY?

WHAT DID YOU LEARN ABOUT SCIENCE TODAY?

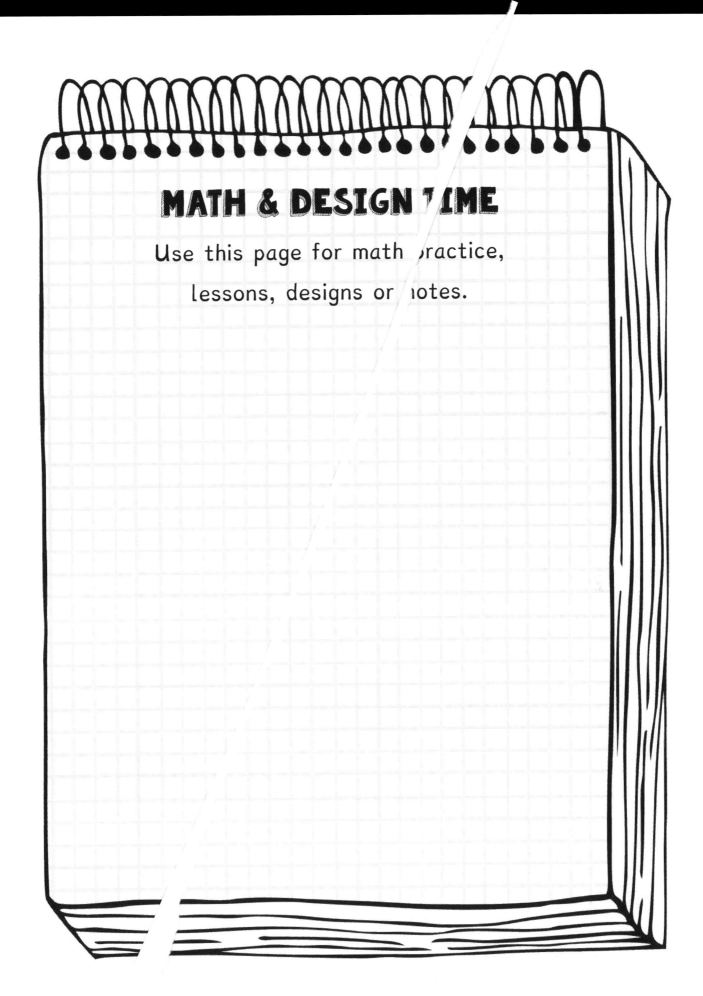

MATH & DESIGN TIME

Use this page for math practice,

lessons, designs or notes.

MOVIE TIME

Watch a movie or documentary about pets.

TITLE:_____

RATING:

CREATIVE WRITING

Write a short story about this picture. Ask someone
older to help you write the words.

MINECRAFT

BUILDING CHALLENGE

Design and build a home for a pet in your Minecraft world, with Lego, or in real life.

Draw the Missing Part

LISTENING TIME
CLASSICAL MUSIC & LITERATURE

Today's Date:_____

Listen to an audio book or classical music.

Draw and doodle below.

I am listening to: _____

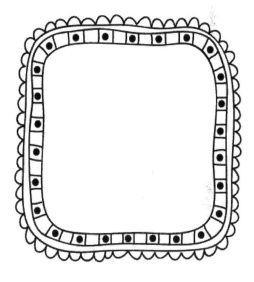

Today's Date:

_____

READING TIME

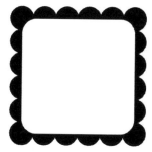

Write and draw about what you are reading.

FIELD TRIPS & BACKYARD SCIENCE

Go somewhere and draw what you see! Look for pets.

If you can't go very far, go to a park or your own backyard.

Today's Date: _____

Today I Saw: _____

_____

_____

_____

Trace & Color

SPELLING TIME

Choose a Letter: ___

Find 15 words that begin or end with that letter.

Five Nouns:

_____

_____

_____

_____

Five Adjectives:

_____

_____

_____

_____

Three pets:

_____

_____

Two Verbs:

_____

_____

Write a silly story, poem, song or play using words from your spelling list.

_____

_____

_____

_____

_____

_____

_____

_____

_____

_____

_____

_____

_____

_____

_____

_____

_____

_____

CREATE A COMIC STRIP

Use your spelling words.

JUST FOR FUN!

Draw & Doodle

CREATIVE WRITING

Write a short story about this picture. Ask someone older to help you write the words.

MOVIE TIME

Watch a movie or documentary about pets.

TITLE:_____

RATING:

DRAW ME

STORY WRITING TIME

If you can't think and write at the same time, record your story or ask someone older for help.

Title:

_____

Names & Descriptions of Characters:

_____
_____
_____
_____

Base your story on the picture to the left.

_____
_____
_____
_____
_____
_____
_____
_____
_____
_____
_____
_____
_____
_____

Coloring Time!

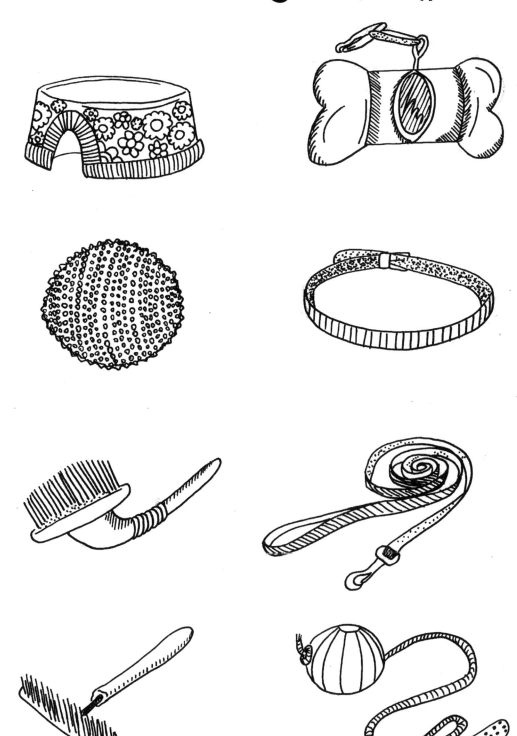

Draw the Missing Part

CREATIVE WRITING

Write a short story about this picture. Ask someone older to help you write the words.

PIXEL ART

Create Your Own Pixel Design

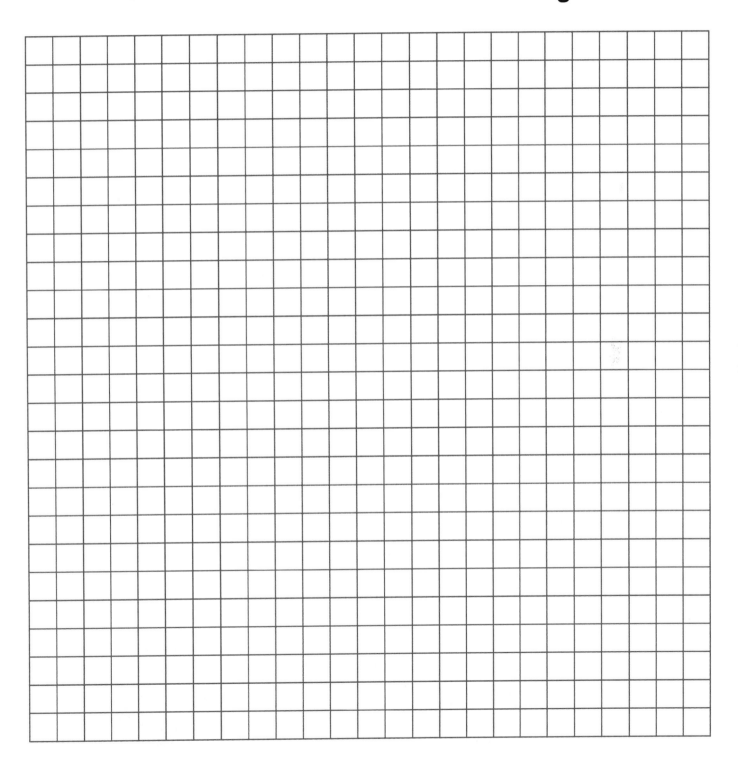

CURSIVE WRITING PRACTICE

Just for Fun!

Today's Date:

_____

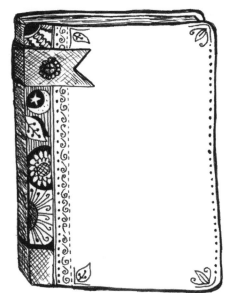

Write and draw about
what you are reading.

FIELD TRIPS & BACKYARD SCIENCE

Go somewhere and draw what you see! Look for pets.

If you can't go very far, go to a park or your own backyard.

Today's Date: _____

Today I Saw: _____

_____

_____

_____

Trace & Color

DRAW ME

PIXEL ART

Ideas & Inspiration

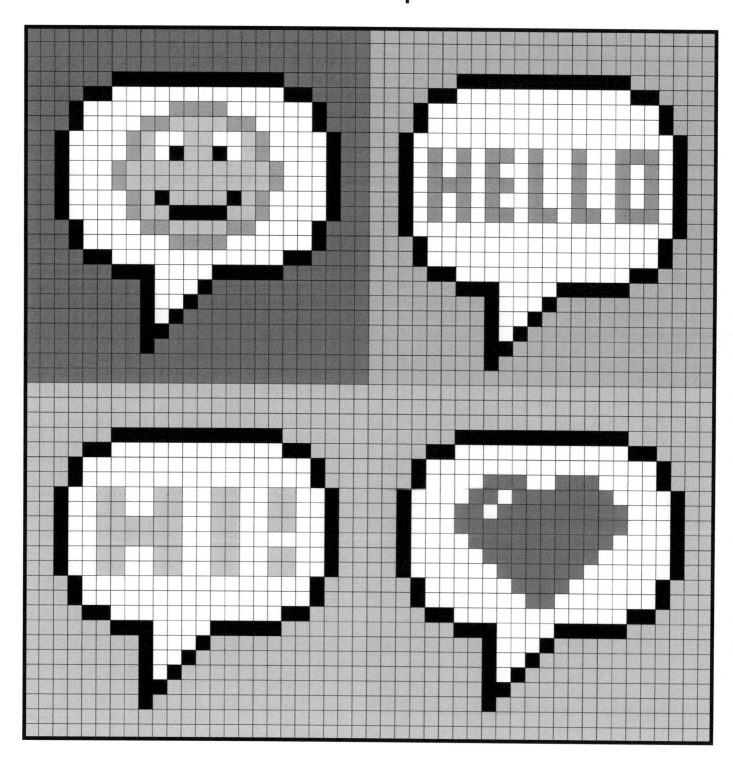

PIXEL ART

Create Your Own Pixel Design

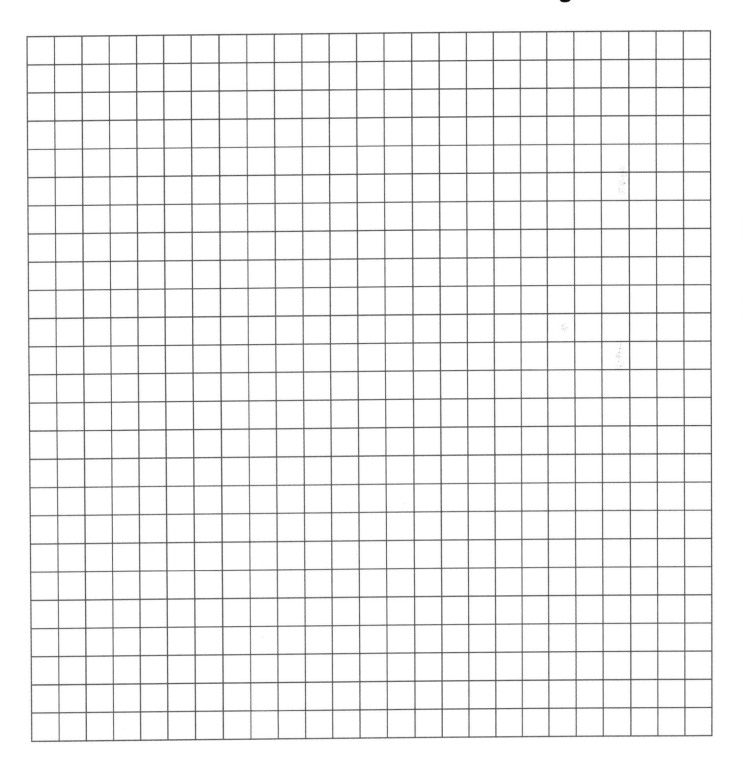

Today's
Date:

TO-DO LIST

1. _____

2. _____

3. _____

4. _____

How are you
FEELING TODAY?

Draw a Pet

DRAW ME

Today's
Date:

TO-DO LIST

1._____

2._____

3._____

4._____

How are you
FEELING TODAY?

Draw a fish

Draw a Pet

Dot-To-Dot Count by 12's

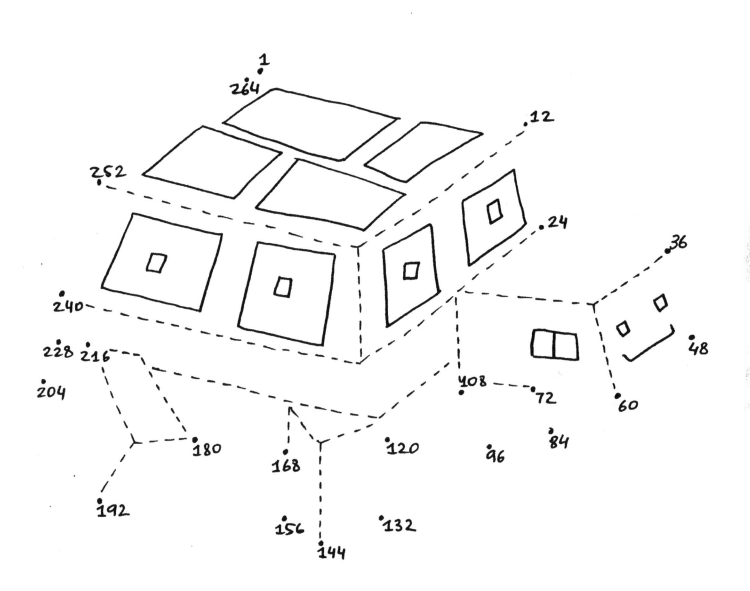

159

SPELLING TIME

Choose a Pet

‗ ‗ ‗ ‗ ‗ ‗ ‗ ‗ ‗ ‗ ‗ ‗ ‗ ‗ ‗ ‗ ‗ ‗ ‗

Look in your books for 10 words that have some of the same letters as this pet.

1. _____

2. _____

3. _____

4. _____

5. _____

6. _____

7. _____

8. _____

9. _____

10. _____

Coloring Time!

Draw the Missing Part

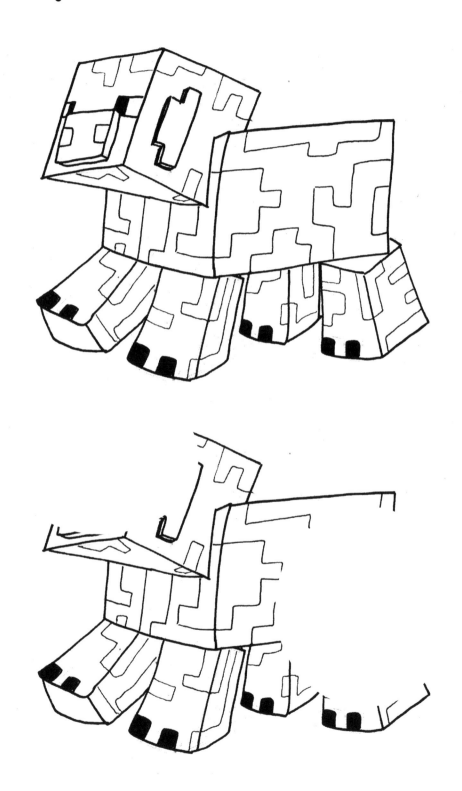

MOVIE TIME

Watch a movie or documentary about pets.

TITLE:_____

RATING:

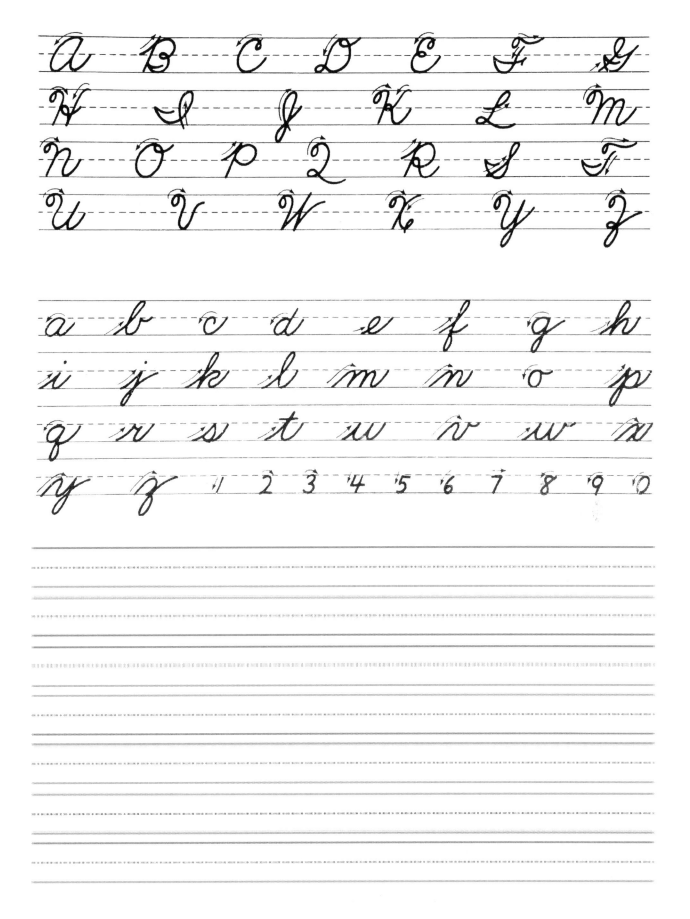

What am I Thinking?

Just for Fun!

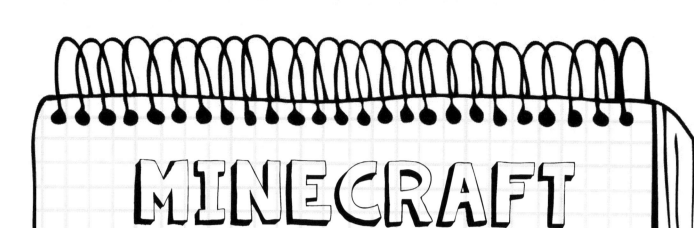

MINECRAFT

BUILDING CHALLENGE

Design and build a home for a pet in your Minecraft world, with Lego, or in real life.

FIELD TRIPS & BACKYARD SCIENCE

Go somewhere and draw what you see! Look for pets.

If you can't go very far, go to a park or your own backyard.

Today's Date: _____

Today I Saw: _____

_____

_____

_____

READING TIME

Today's Date:

_____

Write and draw about what you are reading.

WHAT DID YOU LEARN ABOUT HISTORY TODAY?

WHAT DID YOU LEARN ABOUT SCIENCE TODAY?

PETS AROUND THE WORLD

CHOOSE A POPULAR PET FROM ANOTHER COUNTRY: _____

WHERE IN THE WORLD IS THIS PET POPULAR?

FUN FACTS:

DRAW THE PET:

STORY WRITING TIME

If you can't think and write at the same time, record your story or ask someone older for help.

Title:

_____

Names & Descriptions of Characters:

_____
_____
_____
_____
_____

Base your story on the picture to the left.

_____
_____
_____
_____
_____
_____
_____
_____
_____
_____
_____
_____
_____
_____
_____
_____

CURSIVE WRITING PRACTICE

SPELLING TIME

Choose a Letter: ___

Find 15 words that begin or end with that letter.

Five Nouns:

_____

_____

_____

_____

_____

Five Adjectives:

_____

_____

_____

_____

_____

Three pets:

_____

_____

_____

Two Verbs:

_____

_____

Write a silly story, poem, song or play using words from your spelling list.

_____

_____

_____

_____

_____

_____

_____

_____

_____

_____

_____

_____

_____

_____

_____

_____

_____

_____

CREATE A COMIC STRIP

Use your spelling words.

MOVIE TIME

Watch a movie or documentary about pets.

TITLE:_____

RATING:

Draw Your Favorite Scenes:

CREATIVE WRITING

Write a short story about this picture. Ask someone
older to help you write the words.

What am I Thinking?

LISTENING TIME
CLASSICAL MUSIC & LITERATURE

Today's Date:_____

Listen to an audio book or classical music.

Draw and doodle below.

I am listening to: _____

Coloring Time!

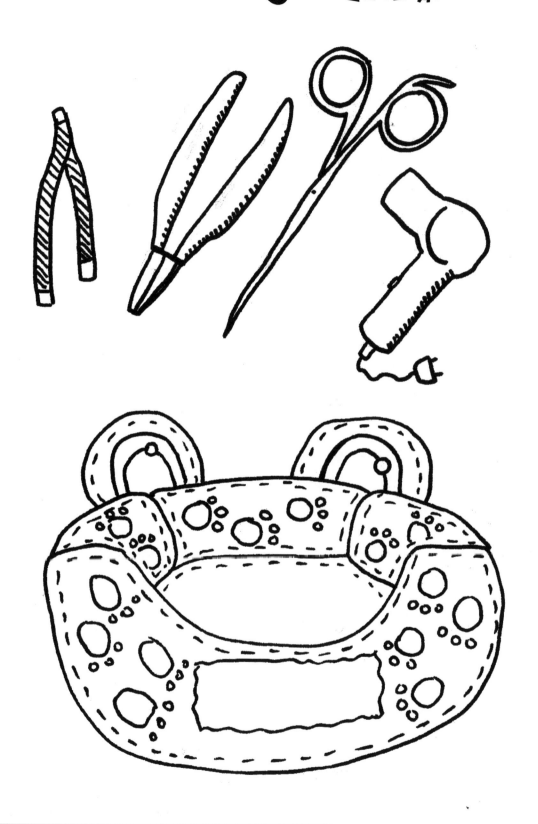

Draw the Missing Part

Today's Date:

_____

READING TIME

Write and draw about what you are reading.

MINECRAFT

BUILDING CHALLENGE

Design and build a home for a pet in your Minecraft world, with Lego, or in real life.

Trace & Color

JUST FOR FUN!

The Thinking Tree
FUN-SCHOOLING
JOURNALS

Copyright Information

Contact Us:

The Thinking Tree LLC

317.622.8852 PHONE (Dial +1 outside of the USA) 267.712.7889 FAX

FunSchoolingBooks.com

LEARNING IS FUN WITH THINKING TREE BOOKS!

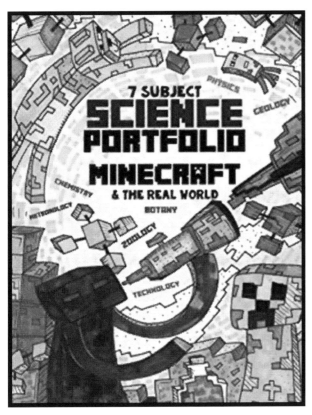

Made in the USA
Columbia, SC
15 March 2023

13804331R00107